DATE DUE

MASTER THIS!

Cartoons and Manga

Des Taylor

PowerKiDS
press.

New York

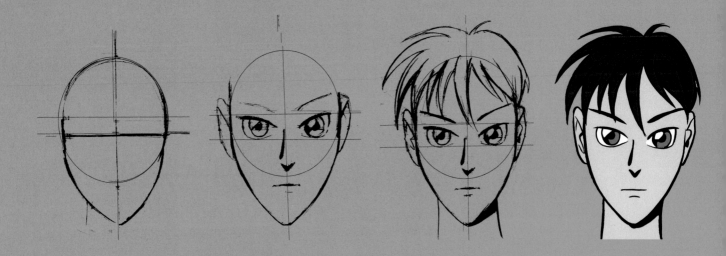

Published in 2012 by The Rosen Publishing Group Inc.
29 East 21st Street, New York, NY 10010

First Edition

Series Editor: Rasha Elsaaed
Editor: Julia Adams

Produced by Tall Tree Ltd
Editor, Tall Tree: Neil Kelly
Designer: Jonathan Vipond

Library of Congress Cataloging-in-Publication Data

Taylor, Des.
Cartoons and manga / by Des Taylor. -- 1st ed.
     p. cm. -- (Master this!)
Includes index.
ISBN 978-1-4488-5283-3 (library binding)
1. Comic books, strips, etc.--Japan--Technique--Juvenile
literature. 2. Cartooning--Technique--Juvenile
literature. I. Title.
NC1764.5.J3T39 2012
741.5'1--dc22

                          2010046331

Manufactured in China
CPSIA Compliance Information: Batch # WAS1102PK: For Further Information
contact Rosen Publishing, New York, New York at 1-800-237-9932

Photographs
t-top, b-bottom, l-left, r-right, c-center
All images supplied by Des Taylor, except:
23br Thomas Schulz, 27b Dreamstime.com/
Pseudolongino

Disclaimer
In preparation of this book, all due care has been
exercised with regard to the advice, activities, and
techniques depicted. The publishers regret that they
can accept no liability for any loss or injury sustained.
When learning a new skill, it is important to get expert
instruction and to follow a manufacturer's guidelines.

Contents

Drawing Cartoons

Cartoons are illustrated versions of real or imaginary events, often drawn with exaggerated features, poses, and expressions to highlight action or comedy. Drawing cartoons is a way of letting your imagination run wild.

Cartoon Types

Comic strips and cartoons appear in many different formats, including newspapers, magazines, **comics**, **graphic novels**, and the Internet. Cartoons come in a range of styles that reflect the subject of the cartoon, whether it shows action or humor, as well as the country where the cartoon was created. For example, **Manga** (see pages 22–25) is a Japanese art style that has become popular all over the world.

Even professional cartoonists use their erasers as they perfect their drawings.

Top Tip

Draw lightly when using a pencil. This is the stage when you can try out different views, angles, and poses over and over again. Any mistakes can be corrected with an eraser before you ink over the pencil lines.

Illustration Stages

Anyone can draw cartoons, but there are a few things you need to know that will help your drawings leap out from the page. Drawing a cartoon usually involves three stages. First, the image has to be sketched using a pencil. Once you are happy with the pencil drawing, the image is inked. If the cartoon is to be in color, the color is added last of all. These stages are usually done by hand, but you can also use a computer to create a cartoon from scratch.

Cartoon superheroes are often drawn in bright costumes and with exaggerated muscles to make them look more powerful.

Three Cartoon Steps

1 Draw in pencil to perfect the style and attitude of your image.

2 Use ink to make your image stand out and so it can be printed.

3 Choose your colors carefully to bring your image to life.

Cartoon Materials

Using different tools will allow you to draw in different styles to suit the type of cartoon. Do you want to draw short, funny cartoons or action-packed comics?

The Tools for the Job

A gritty, action-packed superhero cartoon is often created using lots of crisscrossing fine lines, called crosshatching. To achieve this, you will need pens with fine **nibs**. A newspaper comic strip will feature fewer, thicker lines, achieved using pens with wider nibs or even a brush and ink.

Top Tip

Make sure you choose the right paper for your work. If you are just sketching, you can use any type of paper. If you are using heavy inks or marker pens, however, then you should use thick paper that will not buckle.

Essential Equipment

- Pencils *(traditional or mechanical)*
- Erasers *(everyone makes mistakes—even top artists)*
- Ruler or **set square** *(vital for straight edges)*
- Paper *(any type, from regular sketch pads to special comic book artboards)*
- Inks and ink pens *(a range of marker pens and fine-line graphic pens; for heavy block shading, use a chisel-tip marker)*
- Mirror *(very useful for drawing facial expressions)*
- Colors *(a range of different mediums, including felt-tip pens and paints)*

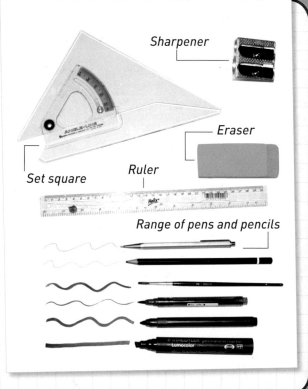

Sharpener

Eraser

Set square

Ruler

Range of pens and pencils

Digital Cartooning

Computers can speed up the cartoon process. Even the most basic computer **software** packages allow you to sketch, ink, and color some fantastic cartoon illustrations without having to spend a fortune. You could also invest in a drawing tablet and pen to make sketching a little easier than using a computer mouse.

Cartoon-drawing computer software ranges from inexpensive beginner's drawing tools to costly and complicated graphics packages.

Perspective

An important concept to learn when illustrating is drawing **perspective**. Using and playing around with perspective will make your cartoons look really dynamic.

Top Tip

Deciding to use a simple or a complex perspective can entirely change the atmosphere of your scene. For example, a three-point perspective is great for drawing a superhero flying through skyscrapers.

The Vanishing Point

Drawing perspective relies on the principle that things look smaller as you move away from them, until they disappear. The point where they disappear is called the vanishing point. Many simple illustrations use one vanishing point, but using two or even three vanishing points will add more complexity to your pictures.

Perspective adds energy and realism, when drawing people (above) and environments (below).

Vanishing point

One-Point Perspective

When drawing a room, you will use a single vanishing point—this is called one-point perspective. The vertical lines of the objects are parallel to each other, but the horizontal lines all head toward one vanishing point.

Two-Point Perspective

Two-point perspective is used when drawing a scene that is viewed from an angle. Horizontal lines head for two vanishing points.

Three-Point Perspective

Three-point perspective is used when drawing something very tall. The vanishing points are usually positioned with two on the horizon and the third at the top or the bottom of the page.

Foreshortening

Exaggerating the perspective in your illustrations can add drama and make them leap out from the page. This is called **foreshortening**. With foreshortening, objects nearer the viewer are made even bigger than usual, while those that are farther away are drawn even smaller. Any lines that form the sides of an object are shortened to exaggerate the effect even more.

Stretch Perspective

In a foreshortened cube (2), vertical lines that should appear parallel to each other (1) are stretched outward.

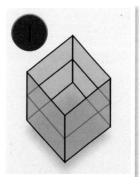
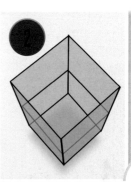

Body Basics

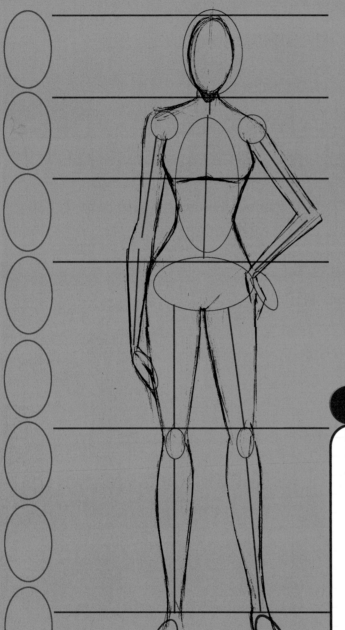

An adult is usually eight times taller than the height of his or her head. The lower legs should be about three heads high.

Drawing the human body is easier than many people think. People can be broken up into simple shapes to help you draw bodies quickly.

Correct Proportions

The size of one object when compared to another is called its **proportion**. To make a body look correct, you have to know the proportions of the parts—head, arms, legs (see diagram, left). For instance, arms hang with the elbows near the waist and the fingertips just above the knee.

Drawing a Basic Body

Start by drawing three ovals for the head, chest, and hips.

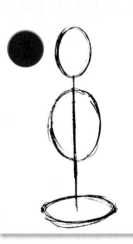

Connect the ovals with a line that represents the spine.

Body Types

Once you have sketched the proportions of a body, you can start to shape it and add details. Before starting this, you need to think about what character you want to draw. A superhero may have bulging muscles. Male characters tend to be larger than females and will have most of their bulk up in the chest, while a female's center of gravity will be lower, usually around the hips.

Draw a shallow "V" shape for the person's collar bone.

(4) Sketch in the arms and legs using straight lines. Add circles for the shoulder and knee joints.

(5) Flesh out the body, adding bulk for the muscles of the neck, shoulders, chest, arms, and legs.

11

Heads and Faces

The face is the most expressive body part and can be difficult to draw. Start by getting the features the right size and in the right place.

Head Basics

Mastering the proportions and positions of the features is essential. The eyes should be drawn about one-third of the way down the face, and should sit one eye-width apart. The mouth sits about one-third of the way up from the chin. The hairline starts about one-third of the way between the top of the head and the eyes.

Top Tip

Copying the faces in magazines and newspapers is a great way to learn about facial expressions. Pay attention to the ways in which people use their eyes, eyebrows, and mouths to show emotion.

Drawing a Basic Head

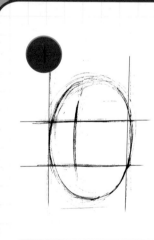
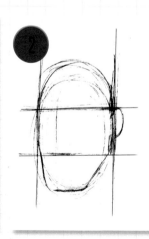

Sketch an oval, then draw lines to position your eyes, mouth, and nose.

Outline the jaw shape and draw in an ear, which should hang from your "eye" line.

Draw the shapes of the nose and mouth and start to sketch in the hairline.

Now you can draw the eyes, eyebrows, hair, and other features.

Facial Variations

When you have laid out the basic shape of the head, you can alter or enlarge different parts to suit the character you want to draw. A male superhero usually has a square-shaped jaw, while a young heroine may have a more oval-shaped face. A menacing character may have an oversized head. Villains may have heavy eyebrows, and criminal masterminds may have a large, wrinkled forehead and shifty eyes.

Expressions

Half of what makes your characters individual are the expressions that form their personalities. Here are some of the basic facial expressions.

Angry

Thoughtful

Frightened

Show anger by lowering the insides of eyebrows into a "V" shape.

Thought can be shown by raising one eyebrow and twisting the mouth.

To show fear, raise the eyebrows and make the eyes bigger.

Drawing Hands

Drawing hands will use up more of your eraser than any other part of the body. If you master the basics, you will be punching out superheroes' fists in no time.

Hand Size

Artists often make the mistake of drawing hands too small. To get an idea of its size, place your hand over your face. The tips of the fingers should touch your hairline, while the bottom of your palm will sit on your chin.

Proportions of the Hand

- The thumb side of the hand is larger than the side with the little finger.
- The hand is broader at the fingers than at the wrist.
- The thumb is set into the palm of the hand.
- The length of the thumb is the same as the length of the middle finger.
- The index and third fingers are usually the same length.

Drawing a Basic Hand

Start with a circle, divided into quarters, to form the palm.

To draw a right hand, draw an oval in the bottom right quarter.

Add another oval above this to form the thumb.

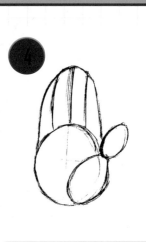

Draw a larger oval and divide it to make the four fingers.

Hand Basics

As with other parts of the body, you can break a hand down into a collection of basic shapes. Starting with a number of ovals and circles (see below), you can create a simple hand shape. To draw more complex hand poses, however, it is important to spend some time studying your own hands. Try using a mirror so that you can see all sides of your hand at the same time, as you form a variety of different shapes.

Fist

Held out for a kiss

Gripping a walking stick

Relaxed hand

Swiping a card

Now you can draw the shapes of the fingers and thumb.

Starting with this plan, you can create other hand poses.

Star File

FRANK MILLER
Artist and Director

Born in 1957, Miller is the author and artist of numerous comic book stories and graphic novels. He is renowned particularly for his dark crime stories. His graphic novels *Sin City* and *300* have been made into movies. *Sin City* (2005), which Miller codirected, starred Bruce Willis and Mickey Rourke. *300* (2007) is set during the Persian invasion of Greece in 480 BCE.

Action Poses

Whether you are drawing a high school sports scene or a martial arts setting, you need to learn how to show your characters in action.

Creating Poses

The key to drawing realistic poses is to get reference. Find images of people in various poses that you can draw. Or you can ask your friends to act out poses that you can then photograph and draw.

Top Tip

It is a good idea to draw a collection of poses for a character if you are going to draw it frequently. Draw stick figures showing your character flying, running, and swinging. This collection is called a style sheet.

Mastering Action

Start by drawing a simple stick figure to show where your character's arms and legs are going to go.

The easiest way to show action in a figure is to exaggerate its stance or motion: swing arms a little wider and kick legs a little higher than in reality.

Viewing Angles

Another thing to bear in mind when drawing your pose is where you want to view the character from. This can have a major effect on the impact of the drawing, adding drama to any scene. Experiment with the effects of varying your viewing angle from drawing to drawing within a story.

You can look down on a character to make it appear small and weak (left) or take a low, "worm's eye" view of a villain to make them appear threatening and imposing (right).

Animated and live-action movies can be a great source of action poses. For a fight scene, turn to martial arts or battle movies for ideas.

Think about the angle you want to view a character or scene from. Sometimes, you get the best result by looking from behind a character.

Drawing Objects

While drawing characters may take up most of your time, you will also need to create objects and buildings. As with figures, you need to get the basics of an object right by breaking it up into simple shapes.

Ball, Tube, Box & Cone

Objects can be created using four simple, three-dimensional shapes—a ball, a tube, a box, and a cone. For example, the outline of a book is a simple box, a tube is used to draw drinking glasses, a cone can be used to draw a lampshade, and a ball will form the basis of an apple. You can then start to combine these simple shapes to create more complex objects, such as cars and animals.

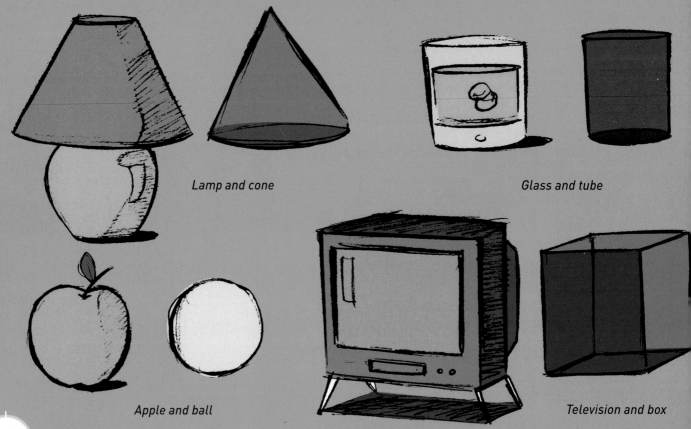

Lamp and cone

Glass and tube

Apple and ball

Television and box

When drawing a complex object, the first thing to do is to sketch the simple shapes that form its structure. A car is formed by a small box sitting on top of a larger one. In each corner of the larger box are the wheels, which are formed from circles.

Now start to sketch in the individual shape of the car, from the curve of the wheel arches to the shape of the windows and roof.

When you are happy with the basic outline, you can start adding detail, such as the windshield, headlights, and tIres. Then you can round off any of the corners to make your vehicle more aerodynamic.

Inking and Coloring

When you are happy with your sketch and you have added all the details you want, it is time to ink over the lines and add shading. This prepares the image for the final step in the process—coloring.

Adding Ink

Inking a drawing can seem scary because it is permanent. However, you can always add to lines to vary their thickness and use whitening fluid to make corrections. Think about the style you want to create. This will affect the tools you use when inking (see pages 6–7). When you start inking, use your whole arm and shoulder to draw the line. Take it slowly—this will help you to draw smooth lines, but not so slowly that you make short, awkward strokes.

Inking Equipment

Things you will need:
• Lamp
• A range of pens and brushes
• Jar of water
• Paper towels for absorbing excess ink
• India ink
• White correction fluid for mistakes
• Rag for mopping up ink spills

Inking Your Drawings

The pencil image is carefully inked in, using pens, brushes, or the computer.

Shadows can be added to give the clothing some texture and lighting.

Coloring

There are lots of ways to color a cartoon, including using paints, inks, felt-tip markers, or a computer. Each method offers different effects (see below). Also consider the style you are aiming for when you decide on your color **palette**. As with inking, the effect you want to create for your final image will decide what method of coloring you use.

> *Pencil or inked images can be **scanned** so that they can then be colored using computer software.*

Choosing Color

1. The inked image holds all the detail and shading needed for the final effect.

2. Computer coloring can create a result with clean lines and striking colors.

3. Felt-tip pens create a bold finish, with thick blocks of bright colors.

4. Watercolors offer a greater range of effects, allowing for more subtle images.

What Is Manga?

Manga is a Japanese style of illustration that has become one of the most popular cartoon styles. Manga influences are found in animated movies (called **anime**), advertising, and even live-action films.

Origins

Manga comic strips date back to Japan in the early 1900s. The word *manga* means "aimless pictures," and the first Manga illustrations were humorous pictures for children. After World War II (1939–1945), Manga cartoons also started to appear for adults. From the 1970s, when anime cartoons were first seen on TV outside of Japan, artists in other countries—particularly in the UK, France, and U.S.A.—adopted Manga styles of illustration and storytelling.

Types of Manga

Shonen—Aimed at boys age eight to 18, this is the most popular style of Manga and usually tells action and adventure stories, often with large battle scenes.
Shojo—This style features less action than Shonen and usually focuses on the story. Shojo cartoons are aimed at girls from ages 12 to 18.
Josei—This is the Manga equivalent of the television soap opera and is aimed at adults.
Seinen—This style, aimed at young adult males, features long fights and some adult content.

*Manga fans dress up for a comics **convention**. In Japan, the Manga comics industry generates nearly $4 billion every year. Manga is the fastest growing area of publishing in the U.S.A. and UK.*

Manga Characters

The Manga style often features characters with large, **almond-shaped** eyes that are usually drawn with glinting highlights. The main characters also have overly large heads and long arms and legs. A key characteristic of Manga comics is cute **sidekick** characters.

These characters may be animals or mystical creatures that have been drawn in a simple style. The lines of Manga art are always clean and made up of simple shapes. This contrasts with other styles of cartoons, which can feature lots of detail and shading.

Female characters have even larger eyes than male heroes. Heroines are drawn with small noses and mouths.

*A Manga action hero has highly expressive eyes and **stylized**, spiky hair.*

*An evil villain may have smaller, narrow eyes, sometimes drawn with an enlarged **pupil** and no **iris**, to show his emotional coldness.*

Star File

HAYAO MIYAZAKI
Anime Director

Starting out as a Manga artist and animator, Miyazaki has won worldwide fame for his anime films. Movies that he has written and directed include *Princess Mononoke* (1997), *Spirited Away* (2001), and *Howl's Moving Castle* (2004). His movies often have an environmental theme.

Drawing Manga

Manga can be easier to draw than other cartoon styles, because the images are simpler and cleaner. The most recognizable feature of Manga is the characters' faces, usually with large eyes, button noses, and small mouths.

Drawing Heads

The head and shoulders of a Manga character are what make it stand out from other cartoon styles. Manga faces usually have a triangular shape. The eyes, nose, and mouth sit in the same positions as in other styles (see pages 12–13), but bear in mind that Manga eyes are usually larger and may become even more exaggerated for some expressions, such as surprise. Manga hair is drawn more simply than in other cartoon styles, and it is usually formed by a series of stylized lines, whether the character's hair is spiky or wavy.

Drawing a Manga Face

Manga-style faces can be broken down into simple shapes in order to draw the proportions correctly. The key features are the wide, almond-shaped eyes and the pointed chin.

Draw a circle, with two horizontal lines just above and below the halfway point.

Now sketch the character's chin shape using a curving "V" below the circle.

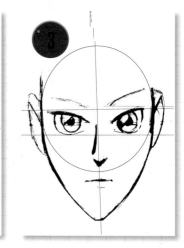

Draw almond-shaped eyes between your two eye lines, and the other features.

Manga Bodies

Your character's body, or torso, is usually formed by drawing an upside-down triangle that narrows to the waist. You can make this torso as slim or as bulky as you like, depending on whether you want to draw a muscular character or a thin one. The arms and legs tend to be longer and thinner than cartoon styles from other parts of the world and lack the massive, bulging muscles that superheroes in many American comic books might have.

Drawing a Manga Pose

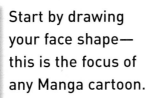

Start by drawing your face shape—this is the focus of any Manga cartoon.

Draw a curved line down the middle to help place the nose and mouth.

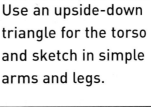

Use an upside-down triangle for the torso and sketch in simple arms and legs.

With smooth lines and elegant shapes, add in the hairstyle and other details.

Sketch the hairstyle using a few simplified, smooth pencil strokes.

Ink your sketch using as few lines as possible, to give a clean effect.

An American-style cartoon of the same pose as above has more detail and rougher, more complicated lines.

Animation

Animation is created by flicking through a series of still illustrations to give the impression of movement. The earliest animated cartoons were drawn by hand. Today, the work can be done using computers.

Simple Animation

The idea behind animation is to show the same character in a series of different poses, which, when shown quickly one after the other, will make the character appear to move. This is where your character's style sheet will come in handy. If you are confident about how your character will look in different poses, then animating that figure will be much easier. Start out by drawing your character walking. The rate at which you flick through each illustration will decide how far apart each pose should be drawn.

Dance Steps

A straightforward animation to practice with could involve a simple dancing character.

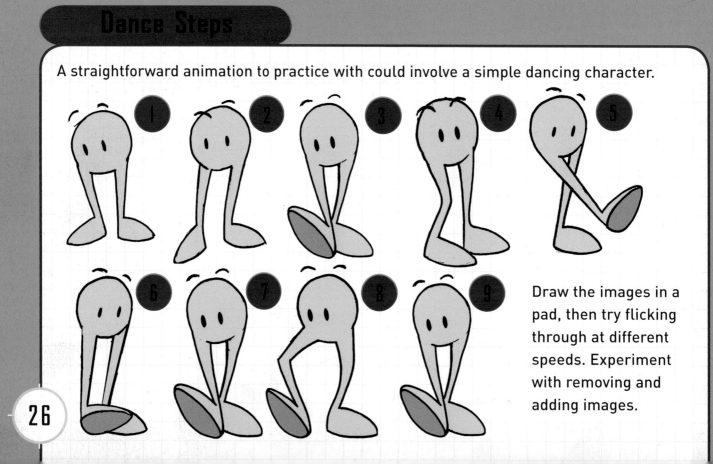

Draw the images in a pad, then try flicking through at different speeds. Experiment with removing and adding images.

Using a Computer

Computers are used to create animation in two ways. Traditional illustrations can be scanned and the images are then colored using the computer and strung together using animation software. Alternatively, the initial illustrations are put together using **computer-generated image (CGI)** software. These images can look very realistic. Sophisticated computer programs can then move these figures to create the animation. CGI animation has become very popular today, with companies such as Pixar and DreamWorks creating blockbuster movies including *How To Train Your Dragon* (2010) and *Up* (2009).

Top Tip

Simple animation computer software is widely available. Some software is even free. Once you have made your animation, you can share it through Internet animation sites.

Computer-generated images are created by sculpting a 3-D net, containing thousands of different points. Characters are then animated by moving "control points" within the net.

Taking It Further

Cartoonists should be prepared to spend lots of time practicing their drawing skills. You might also consider getting a degree in cartoons or animation.

The Next Level

Finding the right reference material for poses and settings can help your illustrations stand out from the crowd. Hunting down references can take a lot of time, but it is well worth it to make your stories more **authentic**. As well as asking friends to pose for you and studying movies and television, make sure you read other comics, since they will provide you with lots of inspiration. Finally, you can share your work by printing it from a computer or by posting your work on an online animation or cartoon site.

Artist Laurie Breitkreuz signs sketches for fans at a comic book convention. Conventions are great places to meet and talk to professional artists.

Top Tip

A school or public library is a great place to research subject matter related to what you want to draw. For the most realistic cartoons, you will need to check the historical and scientific accuracy of your stories.

Many schools offer useful workshops, where a professional cartoonist or animator will help you put together your own ideas.

Study and Training

You can start studying to be a cartoonist at school. Art lessons and design and technology classes cover illustration and computer-aided design. At college level, there are lots of courses on cartoons and animation that will help you to get a foot in the door of your chosen field. Talking to other artists is a great way to learn the trade, and the best places to meet fellow artists are comic book conventions. One of the largest of these is Comic-Con International, a four-day event held every year in San Diego, California, that is attended by 125,000 people.

Getting Published

Professional cartoon illustrators may get work for a comic book publishing house, the largest of which are Marvel and DC. Graphic novels are published by many companies, including Dark Horse, Titan Books, and NBM. Freelance cartoonists can sell their humorous strips to newspapers and magazines. Cartoons are also widely published on the Internet. For animators, there is plenty of work in film and television, using hand-drawn techniques or CGI software.

Glossary

almond-shaped with a wide, oval shape that is pointed toward one corner.

animation the rapid display of two-dimensional images or three-dimensional artworks to create the illusion of movement.

anime a style of Japanese animation influenced by Manga comics.

authentic being believable or genuine.

cartoon a dramatic or funny illustration or an animation. Cartoons appear in print (comics, books, newspapers, and magazines), on the Internet, and in movies and television programs.

comic a magazine, book, or Internet site that tells stories through the use of illustrations. Speech is often given in word balloons, and captions can expand on the pictures.

comic strip a series of cartoons that tells a funny or dramatic story.

computer-generated image (CGI) a picture or animation created by a computer to give the appearance of three dimensions.

convention a large gathering of people who share a common interest.

environmental concerned with the effects of changing and damaging the natural world.

foreshortening a drawing technique that plays around with the perspective in a drawing. Objects that are nearer the viewer are made even bigger than usual.

graphic novel a book in which the story is told through pictures in the style of a comic.

iris the colored part of the eye that contracts and relaxes to control the size of the pupil.

Manga a style of cartoon developed in Japan. Manga characters often have large eyes, big hair, and long limbs.

nib the part of a pen that touches the paper, leaving a trail of ink.

palette a selection of colors.

perspective a technique where objects that are nearer the viewer are drawn bigger, and those drawn farther away are smaller.

proportion the size of one object in comparison to the size of another.

pupil the dark opening in the center of the eye that allows light to enter. It is surrounded by the colored iris.

scanned when an image that was originally drawn on paper has been read by a device and converted to a digital image, so that it can be viewed on a computer.

set square a triangular object that is useful for drawing lines at a right angle.

sidekick a close companion who offers assistance to a hero or heroine.

software a computer program that can perform useful tasks.

stylized when something is simplified in order to create a particular artistic effect.

There are several organizations that can provide help and advice for cartoonists, comic book artists, and animators.

The Graphic Artists Guild provides resources and advice for its members on all aspects of illustration work, from training courses to employment contracts and copyright issues.

Contact your nearest Art Institute for information on classes in illustration and animation. Some, such as the Art Institute of Chicago, offer art summer camps.

The Society of Illustrators in New York promotes the work of cartoonists though exhibitions, lectures, and workshops, and offers student scholarship competitions.

Further Reading

Drawing Cartoons and Comics for Dummies
by Brian Fairrington (For Dummies, 2009)

How to Draw Cartoons
by Mark Bergin (PowerKids Press, 2010)

Manga for the Beginner
by Christopher Hart (Watson-Guptill, 2008)

Web Sites

Due to the changing nature of Internet links, PowerKids Press has developed an online list of Web sites related to the subject of this book. This site is updated regularly. Please use this link to access this list:
http://www.powerkidslinks.com/mt/cartoons/

Index